Laughter the 2nd Best Medicine

(Raisins to be cheerful)

By

Jon Best

I was diagnosed in March 2007 with Parkinson's. In recent years the message from the medical profession to those with Parkinson's has been that exercise is the best medicine. Humour has been relegated to the second division. It is still a vital component in anyone's lives, so I have compiled a book that I hope will bring some smiles and laughter to you and raise some money for Parkinson's UK. There is some Parkinson's content but most of the poems here are of a more general content. I hope you enjoy reading.

Thoughts caper

Inner jester
Courts a smile

Flourishing wit
First impression
Fool's gold

Sometimes even the best medicine needs a helping hand

Universal Cream

I need some ointment
For my disappointment
I need to get some cream
Before I start to scream

I need a safety valve
A real-life tube of salve
Mind out of kilter
Nonsense should filter

Technology saps
Incessant apps
Social notworking
Truth twisting and twerking

Pernicious politics
Using trumped up tricks
Pedals news so fake
Cycle we need to break

Information infection
Truth and hope injection
Before I start to scream
Need antisceptic cream

My name is Parkinson, James Parkinson

License to spill

The Sky Falls

Chicken Licken calls for a hero

A man answers "Number 7"

Double zero

Where is Daniel Craig

Pierce Brosnan or Sean Connery?

New Bond not shaken or stirred

Unlike his cup of tea

His cup is half full and

He is licensed to spill

Diagnosed by Dr No

Stand in Q for his pills

You will die another day gives

Chicken a quantum of solace

Will eventually get there

When he ties up his shoelaces

Just Money Penny
Austerity bites
Spend a penny
Budget so tight

The spy who loved him
Gave him thunder balls
Holds his golden gun
Secret Service calls

The Sky Falls
Chicken Licken calls for a hero
A man answers "Number 7"
Double zero

My thanks to Ian Dury for the inspiration.

Raisins to be Cheerful

Why don't I go back to bed
Take high road to work instead
No sex drugs rock 'n' roll escape
Hits me really dries my grapes

Friday feeling like a blockhead
Trying a remedy that I read
What I need, a sugar rush
Yoghurty raisins so lush

Could be a poet without worry
Raisin d'etre verbal flurry
But what a waste
Yes what a waist

All through the day I plod
If you notice I start to nod
Don't hit me with your rhythm stick
I will try another trick

Do they work? Jury is out
Am sure there is no doubt
Health food good for all
Raisins to be cheerful

Exercise the best medicine, recommended for those with Parkinson's not only for maintenance of the muscles but also due to neuro-plasty. This is a flexibility in the brain that can be trained to help overcome some movement difficulties.

Neuro Pasty (ell of a pasty)

Attended a conference about PD
And heard my best hope was Neuro Pasty
Unable to believe how lucky could be.
Living in Cornwall the home of pasties

I would find a Neuro Pasty with search
Out my front door I set off with a lurch
Ran to the bakers got there and did pant
My heavy breathing caused baker to rant

Had never heard of this gastronomy
Steak and Stilton his speciality
In the next was met with bemused smiles
No luck though with Barnecutts or Niles

Ran to the next to continue my quest
Never heard of it assistant professed
Bacon and leek or how about curry
Lamb and mint. Not now I have to hurry

Again and again I failed to find
This wonder pasty so I did rewind
An L of a pasty was what I heard
Yes neuroplasty a different word

Protect yourself join in some intense sport
Neuroprotection from fitness purports
My bakers sprint though so inadvertent
Served right purpose although by accident

Badminton

More of a badminton player than I have ever been
My skills and talents just have to be seen
I need to remember to bring hand and eye co-ordination
Leave it at home causes lot of frustration

Even when I synchronise hand and eye
Rest of the body wants to know why
It should give any co-operation
When only hand and eye get accreditation

Not king of the court more court jester
If I boast it is only a hollow gesture
Smash at me and I can't get it up
Never won a trophy never won a cup

So when I play do it just for fun
With my dodgy knee on court can't run
Not flamboyant can't play with style
Just hitting the shuttlecock makes me smile

Poles

Nordic walking a new skill
Helps climb up the steeper hill
Needs a little co-ordination
To avoid the frustration

Falling on a hill could roll
If I trip upon my pole
But I will take a chance
Just don't ask me to pole dance

Everyone needs some advice sometimes. You could do worse than ask the four wise owls.

Life's a hoot (with the four wise owls)

See no evil
Hear no evil
Speak no evil
And then came another
See no evil
Hear no evil
Speak no evil
Had a little brother

Three owls of wisdom join
with another of same coin
Smell no evil added to blend
His mischief prepared to lend.

Smell no evil had a masterplan
He would steal a rocket if he can
Smell no evil would go to space
Looking down on human race

See no evil
Hear no evil
Speak no evil
A plot to uncover

Smell no evil used brothers' reputations
To garner his own NASA invitation
Intended to stow away on the rocket
Space agency did not even lock it

The rocket was a drone
He would take off alone
In flight take over controls
Loop the loop, do a roll

See no evil
Hear no evil
Speak no evil
When will they discover?

Plan worked out a treat
Sitting in pilot's seat
Had a while to wait and see
Came prepared with flask of tea

Awoke with start had taken off
Took control was quite tough
Crash into asteroid
Evil smell pants soiled

See no evil
Hear no evil
Speak no evil
How would they tell mother?

Three brothers with big smiles
Cheered at brother's wiles
Had spiked flask of tea
Brother didn't smell easily

They would tell him later
While asleep moved to simulator
His hair-raising journey they mapped
Owl in rocket tried to adapt

See no evil
Hear no evil
Speak no evil
Brothers idea did smother

If you plan to have a hoot
Three wise owls you can't refute
Even smarter when add brother
Talents combine with one other

The Afterthought

I have a friend
With certain charm
Knowing smile
Calms and disarm

Opinions free
From sharp dressed man
Offers advice
Worms from a can

When he's needed
And he's not here
After event
He will appear

Like his cousin
Mr Always Right
This man knows best
Meet Mr Hind Sight

Plenty of Temptation

A Bun Dance

Passing the bakers by
Cakes for attention vie
As I look, they take a chance
Lure me in with a bun dance

It's a waltz for the eclairs
Glide majestically as pairs
Doughnuts romp through the jive
Could believe the foods alive

How can I not appreciate?
Rocking cakes and I salivate
Apple turnovers groove to the beat
Mesmerised I just want to eat

Brownies salsa, iced buns rumba
Stomach rumbles cake agenda
Voguing victoria inside creamy
My mouth waters eyes dreamy

The cakes display just not fair
Even though I waited to stare
One wistful final glance
I escape a bun dance

Take the Biscuit

When life's got you over a barrel
Only thing you can do is quarrel
Life is full of tumbles and stumbles
That is the way the cookie crumbles

When you are left with only the crumbs
It seems like only the bad luck comes
Have a treat open the biscuit tin
Chocolate consolation within

Without cookies you cannot compute
Should have five a day, or is that fruit?
When all you have is a limp biscuit
Maybe just go for it and risk it

Life a biscuit short of a packet
Take it easy you can still crack it
Take a break that will help to fix it
Sometimes your turn to take the biscuit

Selection Box

Chocolate desire
Topic to inspire
Double Decker ride
Have a Chomp with pride

Mind Bounty hunter
Or a Daim punter
Fudge as a finger
Bourneville taste lingers

Mars out of this world
Wurly has been curled
You can have a Caramel
I'll Wispa but not tell

Oh, What a Palava

Oh, what a palava
Owed to a pavlova
Letting loose Pavlov's dogs
Of my appetite

Sweetness desired
Dessert required
Musical meringue sang
Texture so light

Fruit complement
With topping intent
Control it exerts
Dominates by delight

Completed by cream
Tastes orgasmic dream
Spoon cannot relent
Empty bowl, barren sight

Seconds my greed
Did plant the seed
Tasting with passion
Tongue knows no respite

Finally, its over
Led the beast to water
Couldn't stop it gulp
Just felt so right

Nothing is certain

Parkinson's is an individual condition that is so much more than a tremor. It has so many potential symptoms not all suffered by everyone with the condition.

Nothing is Certain

Nothing is certain but death or taxes
Don't want to turn world on its' axis
Things have a tendency to happen as a three
So I introduce a certain bladder urgency

Undercover but can spoil our leisure
With unruly moments of pee-r pressure
Bladder gets old but has childish demands
"Are we there yet?" Impatience at hand

Unlike taxes only need to spend a penny
But demands have relentless frequency
There is no choice an emergency
Bladder insists that it's time to pee

From Skin to Dust

Parkinson's superhero has dandruff as a superpower
So many skinflakes as though had dermatitis shower
Under the hairline my head starts to disintegrate
Virtual crash helmet of skinflakes on pate

Head itchy and sore under the sun
Flakes on lenses sunglasses are on
My chat up lines are less than effective
Head acts as a type of contraceptive

Yet I still live as I turn to dust
Thank God I have yet to start to rust
Won't be as bad after Doctor's review
With the help of a medicated shampoo

Milking the bovine humour

Don't Pat the Cow!

I wonder if you have herd
A cow plot has occurred
They have shed their sense of calm
Revolution on the farm

They are ready for a battle
Beware of dairy cattle
The cows have a beef with you
Their revenge comes with a moo

We have milked the sacred cow
So udderly unstable now
That when all is said and dung
See a bull and you must run

Keep eyes peeled for a surprise
Cows will combat with the pies
Fielded a weapon with no sign
Beware the bovine landmine

Billy Houdini

Over the hedge
Lushness allege
Pastures greener
Hungry demeanour
.
View expanding
When outstanding
In his field
Sees his yield
.
Left open gate
Temptation great
Crop of cabbage
Baa's and ravage
.
Billy Goat Gruff
Will eat enough
Farmers blame vote
To escape goat

Fleet of Mind

Freddie the Fox had fleet feet
So fast no foxhound could compete
For the hunt became a worry
They would never catch their quarry

The head huntsman had a thought
That fox a lesson would be taught
Would be last time given run around
Hunted by a pack of greyhounds

The fox lay waiting in the sun
Surprised by speeds greyhounds run
If they caught him it was the end
Clever fox on brain depends

A risk he took he climbed a tree
Jumped at huntsman horse quickly
Head huntsman with some dismay
Startled as fox dislodged his toupee

The greyhounds renewed the chase
A huge grin filled foxes face
He watched the greyhounds could but stare
Forgot fox, hounds chased huntsman's hair

Lord Fatcat

Easy money if I can

As manors maketh the man

Pronounced the great Lord Fatcat

Being poor is just old hat

He was happy did not care

Had more gold than was his share

Earned it by the others graft

Divest from others his craft

Counting cash will make him purr

Wrapped up warm inside his fur

Outside a shivering mouse

Knocked at the door of Lords house

When Fatcat answered he did tell

Why he came with awful smell

I have a bargain to please

Invest in my new green cheese

Lord Fatcat was unaware

Of this cheese which was so rare

Mouse collected only cheese old

That had started to grow mould

The Lord would not take a chance

To leave a good circumstance

He bartered and he haggled

Until a deal he snaggled

Mouse so cheeky for his sins

Sold Lord contents of own bins

Fed hungry friends wise old mouse

Tricked the Fatcat with his nouse

For my daughters

The Ancient Torture of Being Twisted Around Little Fingers

Dad ,ummm Dadddd
You buy my sisters clothes right?
Yes from under £5 site
I would like a new skirt
Ok that shouldn't hurt
But I don't know what you like
Dad not just any there is one I like

Dads mystical sixth sense
Bangs the alarm gong of doom
To the beat of financial distress
Thoughts of wallet money starved gloom

Dad asks, "how much is it?"
It's not £60 or that shit
Dad gives big sigh
Can't promise no surprise
Until cost surmise
Looks into daughters eyes

Dad has invoked the code
Of wallet protection mode
Leather skinned creature saved from extinction
Should award medal for resilient distinction
/
Later Dad would say
Its £38 to pay
But that's not £60 is reply
With a twinkle in the eye
Anyway it is actually £35 is it not?
No says Dad, "postage £38 for the lot"

Here we leave the attrition
Of this wallet raiding mission
Outcome in the balance
Does Dad even stand a chance?

Daughters of the Apocalypse

Beautiful in appearance who would think
Bringers of chaos what's the link?
I'll help you out and give you some tips
My Daughters of the Apocalypse
The four riders would turn shaking with fear
This trio scares them it is quite clear
The riders can't face them are not equipped
To take on Daughters of the Apocalypse
Rhi is the leader a mistress of rage
Ilona can confuse any, despite her age
Last word Shan is ready with quips
Beware my Daughters of Apocalypse
Do not ever choose to mess with me
I have allies who will always see
Come to my aid and the words on their lips
Don't mess with Dad of the Apocalypse
My daughters work singly but when they combine
An unholy trinity a trio so sublime
I warn you to run and be careful of trips
Or upon you will be Daughters of Apocalypse
They are my pride. My pride, my joy and my love
They are my angels from heaven above
I see their dark-side but whatever hardships
We are as one Dad and Daughters of Apocalypse

Every Man Has The DIY Chromosome

I am a man and don't know why
Genetically skilled in DIY
In my cupboard have the tools
Just follow the DIY rules

Don't read instructions until you blunder
Construction with a sense of wonder
Parts missing is it all here?
Under control don't worry dear

Why are the wires in a tangle?
Why does it tilt at that angle?
I will fix it with my hammer
Surely that's the proper manner?

Next chapter in this epic
Is a story of the attic
Hanging up cascade of seashell
Surely this has to go well

Ornament to hang from a beam
In dining room where it can be seen
Went up above in the attic
Beam disappeared as if by magic

Forgot had gone up much more
Bedroom between on intervening floor
Then it dawned, stepped back to retreat
Rotten board broke under my feet

Wife called to check how I was feeling
As I lay foot through hole in the ceiling
How did it happen what was I doing
Prides turn for fall as I was reviewing

Better the devil you know.

My Time

When it's my time
Will I be late?
Avoid the grasp
Of the hands of fate
Lead the devil
A merry dance
No not to hell
Not a chance
Let me hold
That heavy trident
Calm down son
Be less strident
What? You were
A fallen angel
O dear never mind
Have a falafel
The devil did
Decline his dinner
Not vegetarian
Rather thinner
That's why he had
A toasting fork
Large enough for
Whole pig of pork
And now I made
My first mistake
A commandment
Did I break
I told him that
His watch was slow
He smiled
He did know

I told a lie
Committed a sin
My soul his
Had to give in
The devil had a
Sense of humour
Inscribed my poem
Says the rumour
Written on this
My tomb stones
My bullshit
Above my bones

Devils Toupee

Looking in the mirror
Devil may care
Admiring vanity
Devil may Stare

Noticed for the first time
Age showing there
Baldness is showing
Devils pelt rare

Plucking hellhound for wig
Devil won't share
Incarnate of evil
Devil makes hair

One for Valentines

Legend of Valentine

Roses are red Violets are blue
Mr Valentines here for you
All you single ladies don't give him the finger
He might put a ring on it and linger

A poet with charm to disarm
Wants to share a heart that's warm
Will transplant to you with no donor card
Hoping cupid will bring his reward

Turns names into anagrams of flattery
Reuse lines like rechargeable battery
At speed dating loves to mingle
Never wonders why still single

Has more cliches than red roses
Bad back from devil may care poses
Clears rooms with the miasma
Of an aftershave disaster

Uses vintage chat up lines
That like corked red wine
Leaves an unpleasant taste
Innuendo gone to waste

In a suit out of fashion
More past it than passion
Complete with spare tyre
Has a car he should retire

God bless Mr Valentine
For love he does pine
Maybe he has a card for you
Maybe his dreams can come true

If nothing else he is a tryer
If god loves that can you admire
Where is little Miss Valentine?
Give this man a welcome sign

Though not perfect he will give
Everything while he lives
His love centre of his universe
A love that will not disperse

If you look for Mr Right
He may stand in plain sight
If you wait for Mr Perfect
May just lead to regret

So girls if you want romance
Give a guy that one chance
Maybe he will bring you fun
Maybe he will be the one

Ode to Plenty of Fish

I came to find a solemate
but all I have done is flounder
Have offered free spare tyre
been turned down for being rounder

If they want mussels
Ain't got the abs
Unlike the players
Haven't got crabs

Never fished before where
the fish threw me back
Right type of bait
Maybe something I lack

I only want one
so fishing quotas okay
Get out my rod
Maybe today is the day

I' know that I
have excellent tackle
To boast of it
Could raise hackles

Just one Angelfish
Is all I require
So to be a good angler
I will aspire

Trousers of Destiny

A story I will tell to thee
A story of great joy to be
A true legend you will see
The trousers of destiny

In the shop I first saw
Tried them on with awe
I bent over nearly mooned
Shop girls almost swooned

Put them on pulled up cool
Magnificent as a rule
Trousers would mend my life
Trousers my end to strife

In those trousers I was a star
My arrogance had gone far
Maybe my hubris came too much
Karma decided to keep in touch

Bust a move burst the button
Grab trousers fate beckons
A losers hand was dealt to me
Trousers defined my destiny

The Mission

A tale of courage
A tale so true
A tale of bravery
A tale of derring-do

Just one man
One man alone
On a mission
To the unknown

Stealth needed
Alert and keen
Many dangers
If he is seen

Saunters slowly
Through the door
Nobody challenge
Go in more

See the signs
Memorise layout
Can retreat
Find the way out

Found the section
Need to look close
Moving in
Stay on his toes

What to have
Must check by touch
Are they watching
Is it to much

Strange contraptions
and illicit detail
Will his nerve
Start to fail

Draws breath
Picks it up
On his own

No backup

Heads for the queue
To escape
Next few moments
Success will shape

Final obstacle
Have to checkout
Face the lady
Don't show doubt

She smiles
As if she knows
Sweating now
Head to toe

Pass his card
Give his number
Deed is done
Exit unencumbers

Have survived
Am still free
Xmas present for wife
Sexy Lingerie

Seventies Party

It's red alert a fashion emergency
Send up the flares back to the Seventies
A theme night at a small local club
Return of glam at fancy dress hub

Tartan and glitter, sparkles and heels
That's just the men, wives make up they steal
Everyone groan so high on platforms
Tigerfeet were they ever the norm

Everybody Slade before the spell check
Noddy out of holder yells for respect
Under the moon of love man shows wad
Buys a round as a T-rex starts to plod

A Twentieth Century Boy Bolan us over
Osmand claims to be a longhaired lover
Wild horses guitar screams, air guitar slaughter
As girlfriends wish men had drank more water

The man at the back has a Ballroom Blitz
Drunken stumbles on dance floor grasps tits
Her alarm goes off as she sings shang a lang
Bay City Roller is slapped hard with a bang

All sing along to anthems of youth
In the morning the hangover truth
Blockbuster night although it was sweet
Fashion of seventies would not repeat

New Career

We all need to change direction sometimes New Career 2 is a sequel to a poem in my previous book, 'Shakes and Silverlinings.'

New Career 2

Back to Job Centre That much is true
Vacancy at a cocktail bar is all that's new
The working times they said are such good times
But you need to tell your lemons from limes

Perfect I said cocktails I can shake
After all they can't be so hard to make
A Lady asked me for sex on the beach
Hey steady on my reply to beseech

Martini I could do shaken not stirred
Dyskinesia twists my lemons eyes blurred
Unable to read bottles labels
Took one from the end best guess was able

As I poured it smelled but not much like gin
Turned stomach as well as it trickled in
As tried to read instructions on the list
Head clogged up and became full of brain mist

I put the lid on and started to shake
Then picked up the shaker cocktail to make
As I shook it mingled and then turned green
The oddest martini that I ever seen

Told her it was Martini 007
Undercover but the taste of heaven
She tried it and one mouthful cured her cough
Hey she said this is certainly good stuff

My boss appeared couldn't find medicine
Didn't tell about the drink I put it in
I think he had guessed about my ruse
I was fired as, was not enough Tom Cruise

One job I don't want to try.

I am a Podiatrist

Gnarled toes and sweaty soles
Flakey heels, fungi between toes
Corns and bunions in-growing nails
These are the horrors of my tale

I am a podiatrist
Troubles afoot on my list

Grime under the nails
Hygiene has failed
If only you knew
What feet puts me through

I am a podiatrist
Troubled sole I can't dismiss

Callus and chilblain
So much footpain
Veruca's and blisters
Must help administer

I am a podiatrist
Somethings a foot I wouldn't kiss

Falling arches or gout
I would be without
Not another year
Can't take leg ends career

I am a podiatrist
Job worse than a dentist
Handling smelly feet
I sense defeat

Spice of life

Spice

Are you sage enough to know what's Cumin
Clove at first sight are you assuming
Do you tend to get Caraway?
Parsley I hear you say
It is still in Mint condition
Thyme will tell what its missing
Hopefully won't need Mace
No Pepper sprayed in the face
Salt of the earth it is said
Curry favour instead
Despite it being somewhat Chili
Dill Jasmines a little silly
This rhyme has just been a Caper
Salted with Spice on paper

A Slice of Lunarcy

The moon is made of cheese
If you need a wine please
The man in the moon drinks a claret
He might be willing to share it

Maybe housing the Moon Rabbit
However waxing is a habit
So maybe follicle care
Is removing the moon Hare

The full moon can cause lunarcy
Be careful when you look to see
Might see a cow have a leap
Men in white coats come to reap

The appliance of adversity

Not a fan of my fan oven
My dinner should be loving
Instead it remains cool
I just want to eat it all
Fanned and cooled no heat
Not on my plate can't eat
Casserole was made by Mum
Need it to fill up my tum
Lucky the oven is double
So although its causing trouble
I will soon sit with my dinner
Though am sure I'm getting thinner
My dinner I will be loving
Not a fan of my fan oven

Electric Toothbrush

Old toothbrush almost dead
Brand new one bought instead
Newer model bigger price
What a box did entice

Opened up the large package
Didn't say on instruction page
That while it stood up to charge
Thought it was lighthouse large

Tried to sleep it began to flash
Will ignore it will pass
But that green devils light
Kept me awake most of night

Saved no ships, sleep on the rocks
Wish had not taken from box
Will have cleaner teeth
Tonight's sleep will be a relief

Digger

It is night time not yet morning
There was no advance warning
Outside a mini digger
Six workmen bounce like Tigger

I just can't believe my eyes
Digger much louder than size
Workmen at night is novel
Day spent leant upon shovel

They clatter, clash, clang and bang
In my bedroom their noise rang
Awake due to the commotion
Earplugs 2am notion

The Highwayman

This piece is inspired by The Highwayman a famous poem important because it reaches out from the poet's corner to the mainstream and is acknowledged by people I know, who don't "read poetry" as their favourite poem. This is my tribute to Alfred Noyes

The Highwayman (a modern traffic-er)

The wind a force of nature tunnelling through the barren night streets.

The streetlights ghoulish shadow makers birth intangible incompletes

The road watched over by the darks sentinel bathed in its lunar glow.

And the highwayman came driving—

Driving—driving—

The highwayman came driving, up to the crossroads slow.

He'd a Safety helmet crowning his head and a mobile in his hands

A bright coat of high visibility, with its silver reflective bands.

Boots gleam their laces long, tied with a bow, end with steel caps to protect the toes.

And he strode with a manly swagger,

His arrogant swagger,

His cocky walk a swagger, stars a twinkle as he goes

Over the pavements, boots clattered and stomped on the surface of the black tarmac.

Carried striped cones, spread clones line dancing without steps, crest on chest Cormac.

An invasion of the short striped minions, cordon with omens signs advertising the fates of those who pass.

Fates of those who pass

Planting a light trio to control the trafficking petrol guzzling mass

That morn there was host of automobiles in their daily rush

A convoy of the unready unprepared for his coned ambush.

A highwayman steals time as he strikes a pose in workman's style not so novel

Work-man's style not so novel

A highwayman steals time whilst leaning on his trusty shovel.

Pets Corner
Tom my one-eyed cat is real character.

Tom

My cat has to wear a collar
I can hear his mind holler
The vets was an indignity
Let me out I want to be free

Back to the start of this tale
Tom cat had eye op couldn't fail
Would not get into the pet carrier
it became quite a barrier

From night before had been starved
No meat treats had been carved
Food in bowl his hallucination
Put in carrier for following in

Half way in he did brace
So with effort on my face
Shove from behind hard i did
Across the floor his carrier slid

Until it reached a wall
As I prepared to give my all
Knelt by mistake on his tale
Yelped and inside didn't fail

Tom has an eye for the vet
No sight in it so no regret
Vet had started the rumour
It might start a tumour

Without it he did not stress
But hang on I must digress
Because the collar went on
Gymnastic floor show bring it on

He twisted turned and whirled
Still around his neck curled
He walked several times
It clung a s though a crime

So poor Tom must wait
Until wound sealed it is fate
Hard to walk, wash, sleep and eat
Collared Tom won't taste defeat

Fears of a Clown

Costume of parody
Sparks the slapstick smile
The rumour of humour
Brings calm and reassures

Puns wordplay, plays on life
Euphemisms misdirect
Emotions dressed in jest
Comedies Tragedies

Gagging on banters quip
Cracks show but not so wise
Sarcasms strong shield
Masks jester's inner frown

Doubts double entendre
Delight as fool tumbles
Then stand up to barrack
Life heckles, clown's shackles

Facebook

Facebook what a marvellous invention
Social revolution its intention
Now that we are all connected
Not the fun we all expected

I do not want to see everyone's pets
looking at animals all day, job for vets
Other people's children are always cute
Until they speak then some are brutes

Status makes a political point
usually just disappoints
Biased and lacking in expertise
No surprise they fail unable to please

Then there are those that moan
Cheer up and change your tone
Life is a trial a tribulation
This is normal across the nation

If it's so bad why am I still here
I am one of the culprits I fear
Posts about pets, children and pain
Political arguments just insane

Rhyming or prose it just doesn't matter
Long as you like, come on and natter
I will keep it up all day.
Verbal diarrhoea my way

Comedy Heroes

Monty Python have featured in two of my poems included in my previous books but this one is based on their work outside of Monty Python. The Carry On films are an institution where you always know what to expect.

When the Python Shed its Skin

When the python shed its skin
A new chapter did begin
Towering over Torquay
Just a little bit Fawlty

Flavoured with Basil
Cured and made Manuel
Scheduled clockwise
Bandit Robin a surprise

Michael began ripping yarns
A Wanda fish he did warn
Of future Fierce creatures
Private functions seizure

Eric Spammed a lot
Idle he was not
Always look on the bright side
In his Rutles he had pride

Dark Fantasy Gilliam's thing
From Brazil to Fisher King
Brothers Grimm, Twelve Monkeys
Time Bandits legacy

Graham Chapman's odd job
Yellowbeard no heart throb
Lastly we keep up with the Jones
Blazing Dragons of his own

Circus up and flew away
Releasing talents on that day
Creativity premium
When the python shed its skin

Carry on Life

I remember fondly in the days of my youth
Carry On films full of innuendo, that's the truth
Smutty and silly and loads of good fun
Camp and good natured and trousers undone

If they decide to renew the franchise
Carefully chosen actors would be wise
Army comedy Carry on Commando
Sharon Stone thought but we said no

Carry on Politics would be very topical
Make a change from those set in hospital
Only problem real life funnier feel a chump
Could not compete, real life couldn't Trump

Carry on Referendum could be a theme
A breaksit campaign not what it seems
A winning vote for the great English Breakfast
Cardiac killer beats continental repast

Carry on outside the goalposts
So many shots missed we can't boast
Clinical the word that we use as it seems
Apply to trials of sponsoring moisturiser cream

Afraid the time of Carry On films gone
Their spirit in the news lives on
Take life seriously at your peril
Laugh and enjoy life with a twirl

Sometimes inspiration is hard to find

The Wrong Poetry

Time to write my sonnet
Have got to get on it
Need some inspiration
For poetry elation

Wear my poet trousers
Disturbed by carousers
Yelled it's too early man
Close shave I ducked beer can

But they had started to shout
It was their grand day out
Eating toast I drew breath
Was matter loaf or deaf

So loud that I did fear
Rabbit would disappear
Curses where was the rabbit
If it's loose must grab it

Even the chickens do run
The commotion no fun
Trousers not made for this
Torn with hole like abyss

So back to my sonnet
Just can't get on with It
Wrong trousers wrong poetry
Guess it was meant to be

Its Christmas

Xmas songs are for life not just for Xmas

So here it is merry Christmas
Everybody's having fun
Look to the future now
It's only just begun

Never a truer word in jest
Goes on at own behest
Noddy Holder patent howl
The beat of drummer Don Powell

The little drummer boy
Wanted peace on earth
Xmas music everywhere
Pa rum a pum pum
Alcohol to share
Pa rum pa rum punch

Bing wants an alien for Xmas
An alien this year
Instead ended up with Major Tom
Life on Mars is here

As he steps on a Beatle
Major Tom does Xmas prancing
The war is over
But John I'm only dancing

Wishing for Xmas every day
A wizard to make it true
Out of the darkness
Harry Potter with wand of yew

Wrong wizard but he Woodn't
Let the bells end
Christmas songs perpetual
You can depend

More mistletoe and wine
Christmas jumper worn by cliff
Saved from the last Christmas
As Nat King Coles smooth jazz riff

Snow is falling
Children playing having fun
Merry Xmas from
This Shakey one

It's Christmmmmaaaaasssss

Xmas is a Hoot with the Four Wise Owls

See no evil, Speak no evil, Hear no evil
And then there was another
See no evil, Speak no evil, Hear no evil
Smell no evil, their baby brother

Four wise owls put up the Xmas tree
A star on top very glittery
Wrapped with tinsel the colours so bright
Shiny baubles and the Christmas lights

They stood back it looked so perfect
A plan an owl his mind would select
He would sneak in to see Santa Claus
Where to hide? Needs a plan with no flaws

Smell no evil his mind did search
Star on treetop would be his perch
When Santa came down the chimney
He would be right there to see

See no evil, Speak no evil, Hear no evil
When will the owls discover
See no evil, Speak no evil, Hear no evil
Sneaky thoughts of their brother

Finally it was Xmas eve
Others asleep. Smells time to leave
Downstairs flies up to the tree's star
Perches ready and so good so far

Someone turns on the Xmas tree lights
Gives him a shock and causes his fright
The star is connected to the wires
Feathers stand up current supplier

Dad awake from the commotion
Sends them to bed with the notion
Santa won't come unless they're good
So they go to sleep as they should

See no evil, Speak no evil, Hear no evil
Asleep under their covers.
See no evil, Speak no evil, Hear no evil
Snores aloud from one other

The Stag Party

Outside there was a dancer
Carousing with a prancer
Dasher had best-man honour
Stag-party stopped to eat a donner

Rudolph in Cupid's fixing
Had fallen for a vixen
Heart blazed like a comet
Too much alcohol one vomits

Blitzen strikes drops from clouds
Stag-party rather loud
Curtains part window near
Don't worry it's only the reindeer.

Ossie wins his Spurs

Tottenham Hotspur
Heritage of style
David Ginola
Used hairspray with guile

Waddle and Hoddle
Kings of the Barnet
Secret that before games
They both wore hairnets

Ossie and Ricky
Helped win the cup
Years before Poch
Decided to give them up

Goalscoring franchise
Bought by Kane and Son
Family resemblance
Seems to be none

Hot shot Tottenham
Used to be on the ball
Like Jimmy Greaves
Paul Gascoigne and all

Winger named Gareth
A talent from Wales
Became the real deal
Decided to Bale

Spurs went all the way
White Hart Lane to Wembley
They always need a Kane
Like Ossie knees trembley

Poldark

When Poldark was remade as a new TV Drama, it seemed to drive the ladies into a frenzy. The content of the firs poem here consists entirely of quotes I found on the internet.

News of Poldark

My mower packed up please come scythe my lawn
I lick the screen when I think of your brawn
Old fashioned Mr Darcy looks like a prude
Takes Ross Poldark to create that romantic mood

Twitter account dedicated to hero's hair
Any weirder thing just couldn't be there
Will return historic drama interlude
Takes Ross Poldark to create that romantic mood

Ross Poldark swimming naked flicking hair
Practising for Timotei ad without care
Fans excited but waiting is no good
Takes Ross Poldark to create that romantic mood

They await romantic hero nirvana
A man with a tongue long as iguana
They travel just to stand where he stood
Takes Ross Poldark to create that romantic mood

He will return trailer goes before
All you women brace yourself for more
Try and calm yourself and not be lewd
Ross Poldark will return renew romantic mood

Romantic Mood (Poldark sequel)

Ross met his first love and came clean
Spotted kissing he had been seen
He had tried not to be so lewd
Next series will repair romantic mood.

Along comes Drake looking for a boyband
Removed shirt thrilled ladies across the land
They swooned fell where they stood
Drake not duck stole romantic mood

Good with his hands made love triangle
Pledged himself gave her a bangle
With reverend has a love feud
Can Drake restore Morwenna's romantic mood

Drake pondlife good with toads
Whitworth witless dreams toed
Somethings afoot a sister lewd
Soon will end revs romantic mood

Demelza to a soldier tries to be kind
Soldier thinks of her, making self go blind
Navigator artist poet but is no prude
Seeks to create own romantic mood

In the tale of heaving bosoms and lust
Do what the shouldn't feel they must
However they are or construed
Desire will return and restore romantic mood

My Cornish background has always informed my sense of humour

Born and Bread

Cornish
Born and Bread
Made in Kernow
In my head

Niles and Barnecutts
Helped build my Cornish Guts
I'm half man half pasty
Large steak is so tasty

Try a Cornish Cream Tea
Clotted cream heavenly
Jam below cream on top
Scone treat from the tea shop

Cornish
Born and Bread
Made in Kernow
In my head

Cornish Pirates say yarg
Win the scrum on the charge
Like Cornish cheese so grate
Try dreckly, not too late

Seagulls on unwary swoop
Pasty stealers loop the loop
The sky thieves are a pest
Shit on car not impressed

With the rain wear wellies
Sun shines cone of Kellys
Paradise at Eden
Glass of ale I'm needing

Cornish
Born and Bread
Made in Kernow
In my head

Saffron buns for a feast
Sold out maybe try yeast
Fresh bread with crusty boast
Just crumbs left after toast

More Cornish than Poldark
Trelawny made a mark
Fisherman friends shanty
Cornish Anthem sung free

You can't beat Cornish maids
Respect or be afraid
They can handle a wimp
With fingers born to crimp

Cornish
Born and Bread
Made in Kernow
In my head

Cornish
Born and bread
Do it dreckly
Still in bed

Cornish
Born and Bread
Made in Kernow
In my head

I hope you have enjoyed this book and that it has caused some smiles and laughter. We all need some laughter in our lives.

This is the fourth volume of poetry I have self-published. The previous ones Hope and Inspiration, Shakes and Silverlinings and Cornish Reflections are all very different in content. They are all available from Amazon.

I would like to thank Sarah Barnes for her assistance with proof reading.

Cover Photo by Jon Best
Authors photo by John Whipps

Thank you for reading.

Best wishes.

Jon Best

Printed in Poland
by Amazon Fulfillment
Poland Sp. z o.o., Wrocław